Yellowstone
Early Photographs of Our National Parks

Graham Wilson

Copyright © 2013 by Graham Wilson

All rights reserved. No part of this publication may be reproduced, stored in a retrieval system, or transmitted in any form or by any means, electronic, mechanical, photocopying, recording or otherwise, without prior written permission of the publisher, except by a reviewer, who may quote brief passages in a review to print in a magazine or newspaper or broadcast on radio or television.

Front Cover Photograph: Early photograph of Old Faithful Geyser.

Title Page Photograph: Handkerchief Pool was a popular attraction in Yellowstone's early days.

Back Cover Photograph: Nez Perce couple in front of their teepee.

Canadian Cataloguing in Publication Data
Wilson, Graham-
Yellowstone,
Early Photographs of Our National Parks

Includes index.
ISBN 978-1-927691-01-4
1. Yellowstone--Pictorial works. 2. I. Title.

Edited by Amelia Gilliland.
Design and Production by
   Friday 501 Media Ltd.
Printed in the United
   States of America.

Acknowledgements
The Museum, Library and Archives staff at Yellowstone National Park were extremely helpful and supportive during the development of this book. I also wish to thank my daughters, Emily and Jessica, for allowing me the opportunity of exploring the far reaches of this wonderful park with them.

FRIDAY 501
Box 31599, Whitehorse, Yukon, Canada, Y1A 6L2
www.friday501.com

CONTENTS

THE FIRST PEOPLES	4
TRAPPERS AND TRADERS	20
EXPLORERS	24
THE FIRST NATIONAL PARK	52
THE ARMY YEARS	64
"MODERN" YELLOWSTONE	90

THE FIRST PEOPLES

Indians have lived in the Yellowstone region for millennia. Most researchers believe that when the last Ice Age ended and the glaciers retreated, Yellowstone became a desirable place to live year round. Fire rings, campsites and stone tools support this belief. Arrowheads and other artifacts more than 11,000 years old have been found in the park.

Following the retreating ice, the climate became warmer and drier and a more temperate landscape established itself. Prehistoric peoples hunted a wide range of animals as well as gathered seeds, berries and plants. These early peoples were nomadic and followed the seasonal availability of their food. They lived in Yellowstone region until sometime around 4,000 BC when conditions changed and they were replaced by other Indian groups.

Yellowstone was home to several modern Indian cultures. The Blackfeet, Crow, Shoshone-Bannock and perhaps most importantly the Sheepeaters all lived within the modern park boundaries over historic time. These groups were primarily hunter-gatherers. What separated them from the foragers was their elaborate tool use, including pottery, bow and arrows with obsidian points, and eventually the adoption of the horse.

Portrait of a Plains Indian wearing a beaded feather headress, a heavily beaded jacket and many bead necklaces.

The introduction of horses brought significant cultural change to these peoples. A horse expanded the hunters range and improved their ability to hunt big game such as the bison. It also meant that more members of the community could travel farther afield and with greater ease and comfort. The resulting warfare between Indian groups, particularly the Blackfeet who monopolized a wide territory during the 1700s and 1800s, is well documented and is largely a result of the introduction of the horse.

Many researchers believe that the only native group to live year round in Yellowstone was a small sub-group of

5

Shoshone called sheepeaters. Sheepeaters are relatively recent arrivals to Yellowstone. Many researchers believe the Sheepeaters established permanent settlement in Yellowstone as late as the 1800s. Sheepeaters hunted both large and small animals but their proficiency in hunting Big Horn Sheep was legendary and led to their name.

Sheepeaters lived somewhat nomadic lives within Yellowstone, and even after the introduction of the horse preferred to travel on foot and use dogs to pack belongings. Sheepeaters tended to live in "wickiups," which were circular homes built of sticks that were bowed together to form walls and a roof. They wore clothing made of animal hides that were carefully stitched together with sinew.

Sheepeaters were well known as expert craftsmen. They used antlers strung with elk sinew to produce powerful and deadly accurate bows. They also built elaborate and effective traps to catch large game. Often these meats were prepared with berries and vegetables and dried for the winter months. They also fished with snares and spears in surrounding rivers and creeks.

Sheepeaters remained in the park until 1872 when it became a national park. Colonel P.W. Norris, Yellowstone's first Superintendent, thought the Sheepeaters may deter tourism at the park. As a result, he lobbied for a bill permanently removing all Indians from Yellowstone. In 1879 the Sheepeater War in Idaho resulted in a battle that lasted almost six months and hardened sentiment against them. In 1882 Norris's bill was ratified and became law. The Yellowstone Sheepeaters were relocated to the nearby Shoshone Wind River Reservation.

On the plains the Buffalo had been hunted to the verge of extinction in an effort to starve the Indians and hasten settlement of the prairie. Small renegade bands of Shoshone, Paigan, Nez Perce and Blackfoot sought the seclusion of Yellowstone and several relatively small skirmishes were launched from the park area. These skirmishes ended September 4, 1878, when the Second Cavalry attacked a Shoshone camp, killing eleven and capturing thirty-one Indians. The message was clear:

Above: Indian child sitting on a blanket. The child is wearing many necklaces, as well as a pendant on her forehead. Her smock is decorated with elk teeth.

Page 8: Portrait of an Indian woman at the Crow Reservation in Montana. She is wearing elegant earrings and a shirt decorated with elk teeth and porcupine quills.

Page 9: Mother and child Sheepeater Indians of Fort Hall Reservation, Idaho. The child is held in an elaborately crafted cradle board.

Yellowstone was off-limits to Indians.

Indians lived in Yellowstone for thousands of years. They lived in balance with the environment in ways we do not fully understand and adapted themselves in ways we will never fully appreciate. Unfortunately there are few photographs, artifacts or writings of the Sheepeaters or other native groups in Yellowstone. More unfortunate still is the way these people were treated and the fact that they were forcibly removed from Yellowstone.

Above: Nez Perce Indian camp on the Yellowstone River.

Opposite Top: Chief Washakie (standing in center) with Shoshone warriors and their families. Several teepees can be seen in the background.

Opposite Bottom: Family of Sheepeater Indians in partially covered teepee near Fort Hall Reservation, Idaho. 1871.

Pages 12 and 13: Crow Chiefs, 1871. Left to right: Poor Elk, Sits in the Middle of the Land, Long Ears, Shows his Face, and Old Onion.

11

My son, my body is returning to my mother earth, and my spirit is going very soon to see the Great Spirit Chief. When I am gone, think of your country. You are the chief of these people. They look to you to guide them. Always remember that your father never sold his country. You must stop your ears whenever you are asked to sign a treaty selling your home. A few years more and white men will be all around you. They have their eyes on this land. My son, never forget my dying words. This country holds your father's body. Never sell the bones of your father and your mother.

Chief Joseph, on his deathbed to his son. He died in exile at the Colville Reservation in Washington State in 1904. He is remembered as a great humanitarian and peacemaker.

Above: A group of Bannock Indians, including Chief Buffalo Horn (on horseback on far left). Buffalo Horn was an energetic and inspirational leader of the Bannock Indians during the 1870s.

Opposite: Thunder Coming from the Water up Over the Land *commonly known as Chief Joseph of the Nez Perce Indians.*

Page 16: Nez Perce Indian couple in front of their teepee.

Page 17: Bannock Indian man wrapped in a trade blanket.

Opposite: A Sheepeater Indian woman reputed to be 115 years old.

Above: Woman and children Sheepeater Indians in front of a wickiup *on the Fort Hill Reservation. 1872.*

They were all neatly clothed in dressed deer and sheepskins of the best quality and seemed perfectly happy.
Osbourne Russell, 1835.

TRAPPERS AND TRADERS

The first non-natives to enter the Yellowstone region were trappers. Throughout the Rocky Mountains, beaver, otter and other animals were being sought for their fur. On the plains, bison were being slaughtered to the verge of extinction. Yellowstone was ignored because of its inaccessibility and the battles with the Blackfoot and other Indian nations.

The first trapper to enter Yellowstone was likely John Colter. He was a veteran of the legendary Lewis and Clark expedition and was considered an extremely capable mountain man. His work with Manuel Lisa and the Missouri Fur Trading Company led him to Yellowstone. Colter traded with the Indians of the Yellowstone region. Colter is best remembered for an epic 500-mile journey through the mountains during the winter alone and on foot to trade in Yellowstone.

Colter lived an adventurous life and had many close brushes with death. Once he was captured by Blackfoot Indians who had a long tradition of hunting in Yellowstone. The Blackfoot stripped him of his supplies and clothing and released him. They then chased Colter, challenging him to run for his life. Colter lived to tell the story.

Jim Bridger was an infamous mountain man known for his exploits in the mountains of the West and his tendency to tell tall tales.

Other trappers such as George Drouillard and members of the Canadian North West Company and later the Hudson's Bay Company soon followed. By 1822 interest in fur trapping in the Rocky Mountains resulted in General William Ashley recruiting a large group of men to explore the Yellowstone region. While this expedition did not enter the present-day park boundaries, it did expose the region to broad scrutiny and this effort had significant effect. Trappers such as Joe Meek, Osborne Russell, Warren Angus Ferris, Daniel Potts and the legendary story-teller James Bridger can be credited with the "opening-up" of Yellowstone.

Above: Drawing of a French Canadian trapper.

Opposite: Illustration of Jim Bridger.

James Bridger was a legendary trapper and told colorful stories of the Yellowstone wilderness that became known as "Bridger stories." In one Bridger story he described going to bed by yelling across a canyon so big that the echo woke him the next morning. In another story he described petrified trees that "...perched petrified birds...singing petrified songs." Camp living was stressful and Bridger's stories helped break the monotony of camp life.

By the 1840s, the period of trapping and trading in Yellowstone had ended due to changing fashions and a reduced demand for furs. The beaver hat went out of style, and without high fur prices the trappers left. Yellowstone was once again ignored and the Sheepeaters quietly resumed their traditional lifestyle.

The deep gloom of the forest in the spectral light revealed on all sides of me a compact and unending growth of trunks and an impervious canopy of somber foliage; the shrieking of night-birds; the supernaturally human scream of the mountain lion; the prolonged howl of the wolf, made me insensible to all other forms of suffering.
Truman Everts, 1871.

EXPLORERS

The 1870s were a period of great change for Yellowstone. The California Gold Rush and the conclusion of the Civil War brought greater attention to the West and characterized it as one of last great "frontiers." Yellowstone had remained somewhat ignored because of its mountainous and inaccessible geography. Also, the skirmishes with Indians had persisted for decades and many plains Indians sought refuge in Yellowstone and it's surrounding regions. Trappers and prospectors had visited parts of Yellowstone, but it was not until profile expeditions, survey parties and photographers visited that Yellowstone gained notoriety.

The first significant expedition was mounted by Folsom, Cook and Peterson in 1869. They were followed in 1870 by the Washburn, Langford and Doane expedition and in 1871 and 1872 by the Hayden Survey. These expeditions all experienced great adventures and misadventures in Yellowstone. For instance, when Truman Everts went missing in Yellowstone from the Washburn, Langford and Doane expedition a search was launched. Everts was found thirty-seven days later weighing only fifty pounds. He was scalded and frost bitten and crawling on the ground muttering incoherently. His story of survival became popular and contributed to the mystique of Yellowstone.

N.P. Langford of the Hayden Survey Party.

These expeditions had many things in common. They often relied on army escorts as they were travelling on land that had not been settled. The plains Indians had been at war with the US and many roaming bands had sought refuge in the mountains around Yellowstone. The bison had been hunted to the verge of extinction on the plains and one of the last herds was in Yellowstone. The rich elk, deer and sheep populations also were incentives for refuge in Yellowstone. The expeditions often used well-trodden Indian trails and relied on the expert advice of the Indians they met.

These expeditions explored the Yellowstone region and put to rest the many myths of the region. In the aftermath of the Civil War there was great interest in the West and resources were spent trying to survey these vast lands. The expeditions created reliable maps, took temperature readings of the geysers and hot springs, measured the heights of canyons and made other empirical measurements.

The expedition team was composed of scientists, naturalists, artists, clergy, packers, and hunters and represented a broad background of education and social standing. The fact that artists were included held great influence on the future of Yellowstone. It was landscape artist Thomas Morin and the photographer William Henry Jackson who first brought attention to the park. Up to this point only wood-cut prints and engravings, which were sometimes based on second and third-hand information, were published. But Morin's grand paintings and the new medium of photography were seen to accurately portray Yellowstone. In this sense, these pictures could not lie and the park held attributes of great curiosity and beauty.

Morin and Jackson's work was printed in magazines and books and placed on display for the public to view. Europe had its gothic architecture and art but the US had one of the greatest scenic wonders of the world. And even though many would never visit Yellowstone in person, they could hold stereoscopes and prints of its natural wonders.

The explorers were largely people of influence who would not be easily dismissed. Magazines published articles about the natural wonders of Yellowstone and had pictures, maps and detailed information to back their claims. The world was discovering Yellowstone through the popular press and nobody could argue with her singular impressiveness and grandeur. In many respects a star was born and her name was Yellowstone.

Above: Members of the Hayden Survey Party packing a mule.

...the wolf scents us afar and the mournful cadence of his howl adds to our sense of solitude. The roar of the mountain lion awakes the sleeping echoes of the adjacent cliffs and we hear the elk whistling in every direction...
David Folsom, 1869.

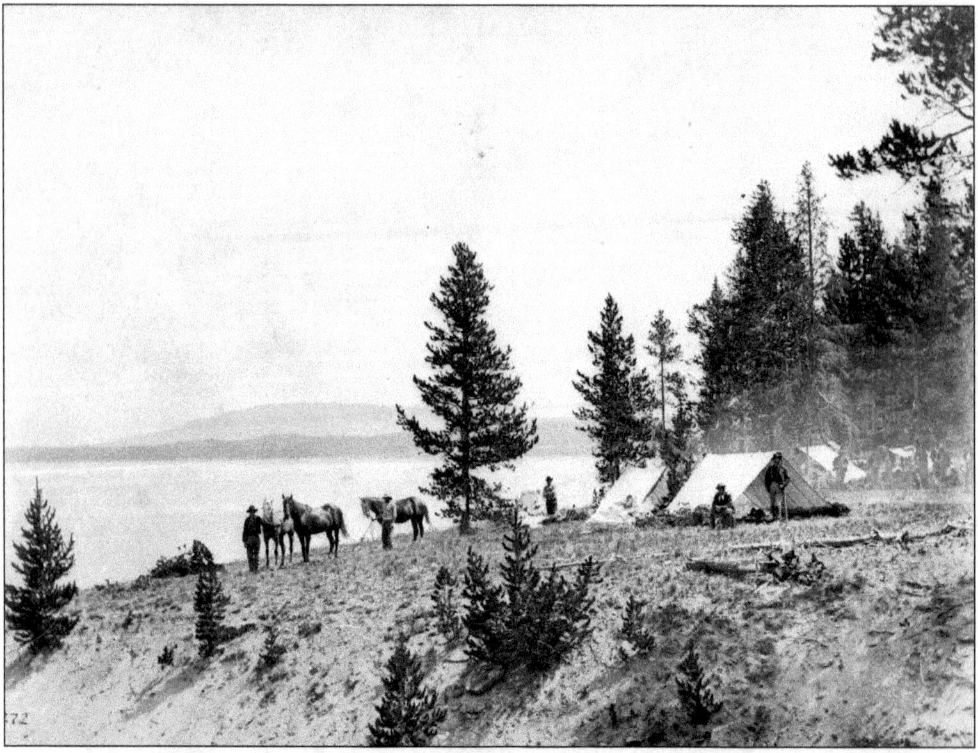

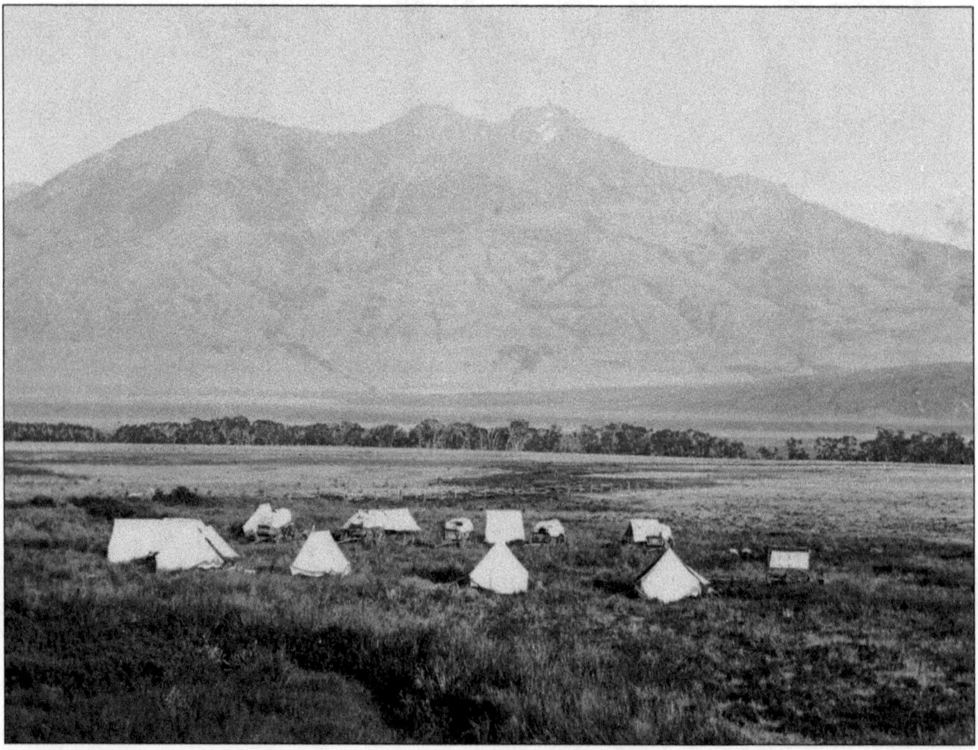

Opposite Top: Hayden Survey Party camp on southwest arm of Yellowstone Lake.

Opposite Bottom: Hayden Survey Party camp at Emigrant Peak.

Above: Ferdinand V. Hayden (sitting on box) and his assistant, artist Walter Paris.

Grand, glorious, and magnificent was the scene as we looked upon it from Washburn's summit. No pen can write it—no language describe it.
General W.E. Strong, 1875.

The intelligent American will one day point on the map to this remarkable district with the conscious pride that it has not its parallel on the face of the globe.
Ferdinand V. Hayden, 1872.

Above: James Stevenson and Henry W. Elliot aboard "Annie." It was the first boat ever launched on Yellowstone Lake. The Annie *was only 12 feet long by 3-1/2 feet wide, 1871.*

Above: Yellowstone Lake near the outlet looking south.

I adopted an 8 X 10 camera... As Dr. Hayden wanted quick publication, we took along the necessary supplies for making prints in the field, such as Albumen paper, silver baths, and toning solutions.
William Henry Jackson, 1871.

Opposite and Above: Tower Creek and the spectacular Tower Falls.

This is probably the most remarkable region of natural wonders in the world; and, while we already have our Niagara and Yosemite, this new field of wonders should be at once withdrawn from occupancy, and set apart as a public National Park for the enjoyment of the American people for all time.
Nathaniel P. Langford, 1871.

Opposite: Lower Falls of the Yellowstone River.

Above: Tower Falls.

Standing near the margin of the Lower Falls, and looking down the canyon...the whole presents a picture that would be difficult to surpass in nature. Mr. Thomas Moran, a celebrated artist...exclaimed with a kind of regretful enthusiasm that these beautiful tints were beyond the reach of human art.
Ferdinand V. Hayden, 1871.

Soon after reaching camp a tremendous rumbling was heard, shaking the ground in every direction, and soon a column of steam burst forth from a crater near the edge of the east side of the river. Following the steam, arose, by a succession of impulses, a column of water, apparently six feet in diameter, to a height of 200 feet, while the steam ascended a thousand feet or more...We called this the Grand Geyser, for its poser seemed greater than any other of which we obtained any knowledge in the valley.
Ferdinand V. Hayden, 1871.

Above: White Dome Geyser.

Opposite: First photograph ever taken of Old Faithful geyser as it erupts, 1883.

Pages 38 and 39: Artist Thomas Moran at Mammoth Terrace.

Opposite: Superintendent Langford on the calcite terraces at Mammoth Hot Springs. These springs had water until the late 1970s, but are now dry.

Above: Eruption of Giantess Geyser.

In the chill mist of early morning, we passed like ghosts along a rude road into the geyser basin...the trail had disappeared and we were treading a crust that sounded hollow and was hot to touch. I dismounted and led my horse carefully around the thin places for fear he would break through and scald his legs...at this time there were practically no trails in the park aside from game trails, only a rough track connecting the geyser basin with Mammoth Hot Springs.
Luther Kelly, 1878.

Opposite: Artist Thomas Moran at Liberty Cap.

Above: Soda Butte in distance.

Pages 44 and 45: Fan geyser on the Firehole River.

This is probably the most remarkable region of natural wonders in the world; and, while we already have our Niagara and Yosemite, this new field of wonders should be at once withdrawn from occupancy, and set apart as a public National Park for the enjoyment of the American people for all time.
Nathaniel P. Langford, 1871.

Among so many wonders it had almost escaped notice. While we were at breakfast a column of water entirely filling the crater shot from it, we found it to be 219 feet in height. We named it the 'Beehive.'
Ferdinand V. Hayden, 1871.

Above: *Crater of Giant Geyser.*

Opposite: *Eruption of Lone Star Geyser.*

Above: Black Sand Pool.

...*the park is full of exciting wonders. The wildest geysers in the world, in bright, triumphant bands, are dancing and singing in it amid thousands of boiling springs, beautiful and awful, their basins arrayed in gorgeous colors like gigantic flowers; and hot paint-pots, mud springs, mud volcanoes, mush and broth caldrons whose contents are of every color and consistency, splash and heave and roar in bewildering abundance.*
John Muir, 1898.

Above: Upper Fire Hole from Old Faithful Crater.

Climb the mountains and get their good tidings. Nature's peace will flow into you as sunshine flows into trees. The winds will blow their own freshness into you, and the storms their energy, while cares will drop off like autumn leaves.
John Muir, 1898.

...is hereby reserved and withdrawn from settlement, occupancy, or sale...and dedicated and set apart as a public park or pleasuring-ground for the benefit and enjoyment of the people...
Yellowstone National Park Act, 1872.

Above: Soldiers from 25th Infantry posed on Minerva Terrace with their bicycles laden with provisions. This was part of an experiment of using bicycles in the military.

The air is electric and full of ozone, healing, reviving, exhilarating, kept pure by frost and fire, while the scenery is wild enough to awaken the dead.
John Muir, 1898.

THE FIRST NATIONAL PARK

Many credit Yellowstone with being the world's first national park. While there were large municipal parks in cities around the world, such as Central Park in New York City, the concept of national parks was new when the Yellowstone National Park Act was ratified in 1872. The "Park Idea" soon spread around the world as governments tried to draw attention to their own natural wonders.

In the 1870s Yellowstone was essentially a pristine wilderness. Aside from small bands of Indians, it was largely unsettled and there were not any existing mining or logging operations. Many have speculated that Yellowstone's fate would have been different had prospectors found gold or other minerals in the creeks or mountains of the region.

The Hayden Expedition is credited with making the first suggestion that Yellowstone was unique and deserved special protection. While camped at the confluence of the Firehole and Gibbon River, Nathaniel P. Langford proposed that Yellowstone become a national park. These sentiments would be included in Hayden's 500 page expedition report and ensuing magazine and newspaper articles. Stereoscopes soon carried depictions of the geysers, waterfalls and other splendors of Yellowstone and within months Yellowstone was on the tongue of millions.

Eruption of Old Faithful Geyser.

At this time, the concept of protecting natural wonders from human development was a prevalent sentiment. Niagara Falls was an extremely popular tourist destination in the 1800s and many felt that commercialism had ruined its splendor. Bars, restaurants and curio shops competed for tourists throughout the area and some feared a similar fate for Yellowstone.

In other areas people were suggesting a concept similar to national parks. In California, for instance, the Yosemite region had been transferred to the jurisdiction of the

state. The Yosemite Grant of 1864 was close to national park status when it stated "...the premises shall be held for public use, resort, and recreation; shall be inalienable." Langford was aware of the Yosemite Grant when he suggested Yellowstone National Park.

The Hayden Expedition had a powerful team in Thomas Moran and Jackson. Moran's paintings and Jackson's photographs captured the spectacular qualities of Yellowstone. Their art was widely published and distributed and greatly influenced Congress. Few could argue with the uniqueness and grandeur that was captured in their images. This fired peoples' imaginations and led to a popular plea to set aside these wild lands for recreational and largely non-consumptive use.

Politicians debated in Washington and on March 1, 1872, established Yellowstone National Park. The world's first national park was born, and the debate over balancing wilderness with development began almost immediately.

Above: Organizing ECW Camp number one, which was the first camp in Yellowstone.

Opposite: Mammoth Campground, 1922.

The hotel at the Upper Geyser Basin was chiefly of canvas, walls and roof; and to sleep there must have made you intimately acquainted with how your neighbors were passing the night.
Owen Wister, 1887.

I have been through the Yellowstone National Park in a buggy, in the company of an adventurous old lady from Chicago and her husband, who disapproved of the scenery as being "ungodly." I fancy it scared them.
Rudyard Kipling, 1889.

Above: Picnic near Upper Geyser Basin.

Opposite Top and Bottom: Tourists wading in Great Fountain Geyser.

Pages 58 and 59: Tourists hiking in Grand Canyon of the Yellowstone.

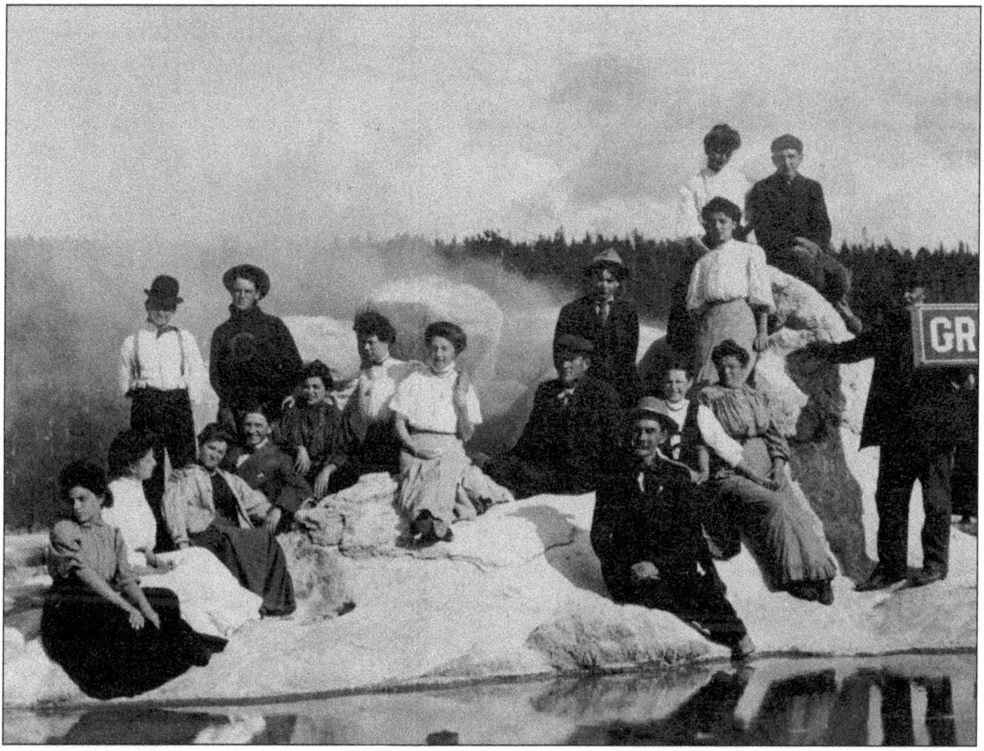
GR

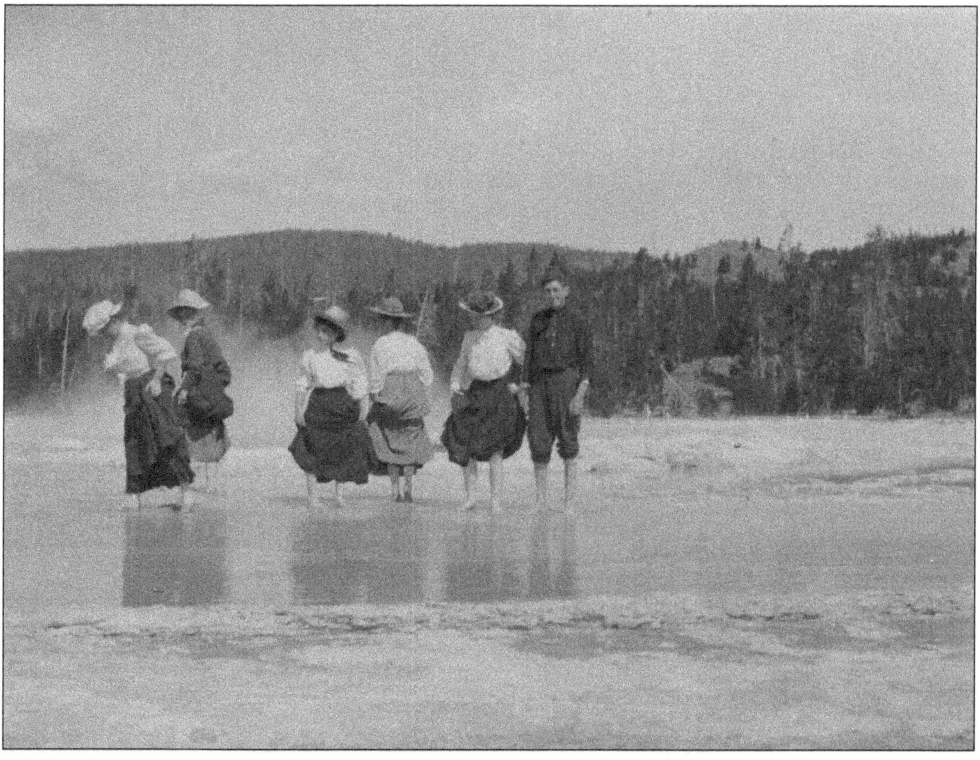

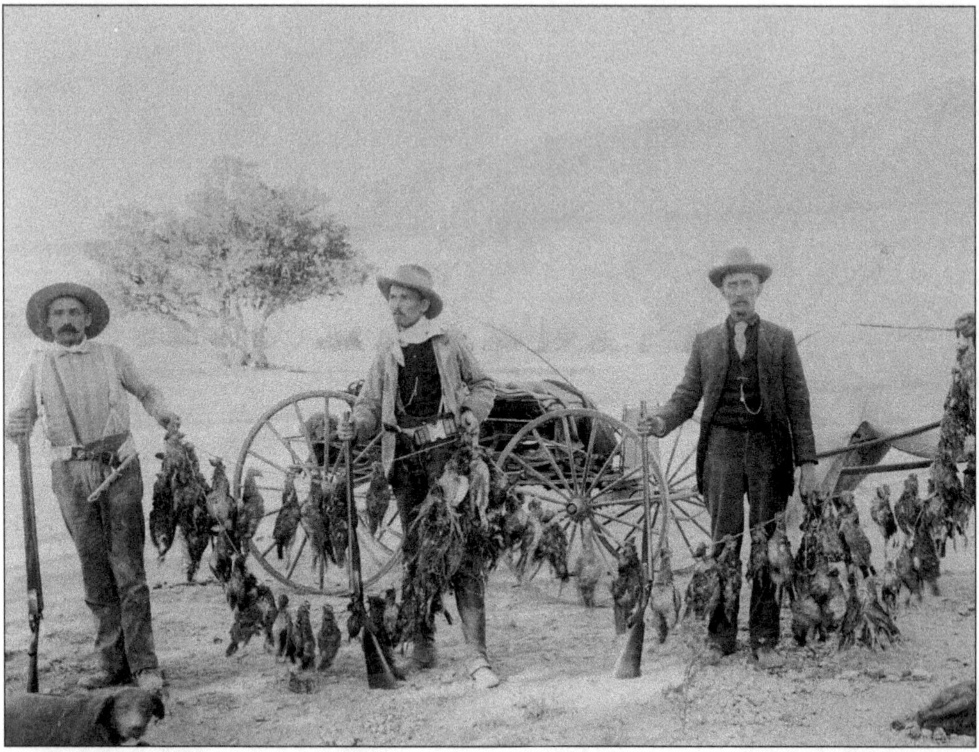

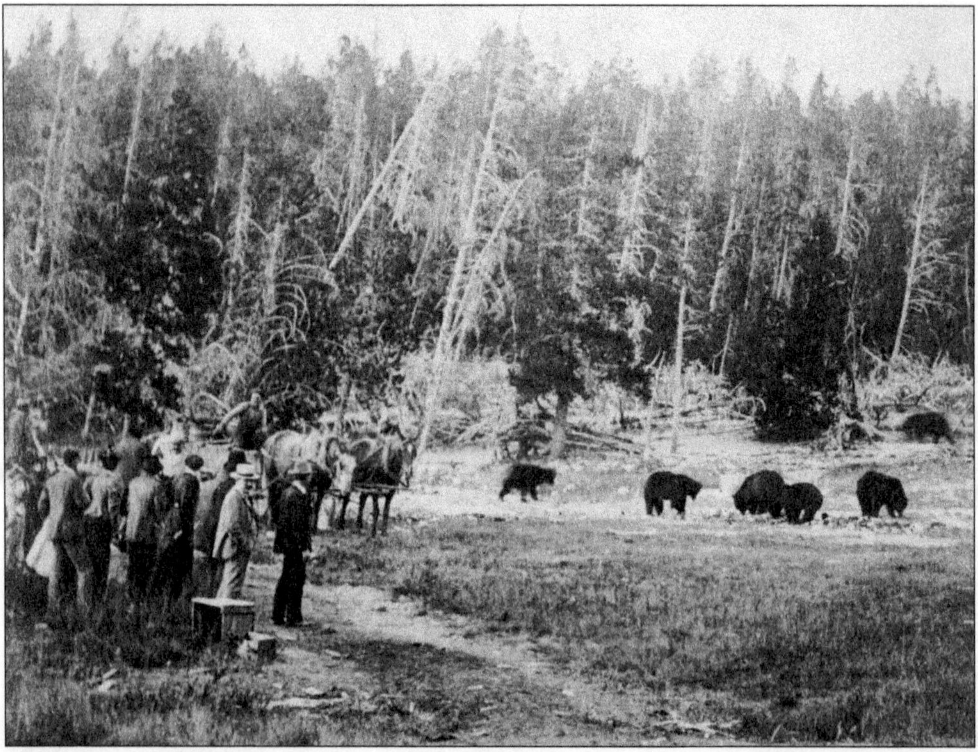

Opposite Top: Hunters with dogs and almost a hundred grouse.

Opposite Bottom: A popular attraction at many Yellowstone hotels was the evening feeding of bears.

Above: President Theodore Roosevelt in Yellowstone.

Of course, among the thousands of tourists, there is a percentage of thoughtless and foolish people; and when such people go out in the afternoon to look at the bears feeding they occasionally bring themselves into jeopardy by some senseless act. The black bears and the cubs of the bigger bears can readily be driven up trees, and some of the tourists occasionally do this. Most of the animals never think of resenting it; but now and then one is run across which has its feelings ruffled by the performance.
Theodore Roosevelt, 1914.

The new road passes through the Hoodoo region, which could only be imperfectly seen from the old road to the Golden Gate. At one time, when James L. Galen, a Helena man, passed through a narrow picturesque cleft, he exclaimed, "Why, this is the Silver Gate!" And so it remained called. All Park tourists must now pass through the Silver Gate before entering the Golden Gate.
Livingston Enterprise, 1899.

Above: The Golden Gate bridge on the Mammoth-to-Norris Road was originally built from wood in 1885 by the US Corps of Engineers. Originally this trestle bridge was more than two hundred feet long and allowed stage coaches to pick up rail passengers at Mammoth and access the interior of the park.

Above: Lt. Kingman of the US Engineers and family camping in Yellowstone. Hammocks were popular additions for many camping trips.

Americans have a national treasure in the Yellowstone Park, and they should guard it jealously. Nature has made her wildest patterns here, has brought the boiling waters from her greatest depths to the peaks which bear eternal snow, and set her masterpiece with pools like jewels. Let us respect her moods, and let the beasts she nurtures in her bosom live, and when the man from Oshkosh writes his name with a blue pencil on her sacred face, let him spend six months where the scenery is circumscribed and entirely artificial.
Frederic Remington, Artist, 1893.

THE ARMY YEARS

Nathaniel P. Langford was the first superintendent of Yellowstone National Park and he had his work cut out for him. Almost everything he did had no precedent. Not only did he and his staff lack experience, but they were under funded as well. These conditions benifitted the unscrupulous and Yellowstone became a favorite haunt of poachers and souvenir seekers who collected and hocked anything they could sell.

By 1886 concerned citizens, park officials, and politicians began to protest the impact of the poachers and vandals that were destroying Yellowstone. Congress was aware of the situation but did not allocate any new funds to remedy the situation. In desperation, Superintendent Philetus W. Norris, Langford's replacement, requested the help of the US army to bring order to Yellowstone. The Secretary of War responded in 1886 by sending the calvary and establishing Camp Sheridan at Mammoth Hot Springs as a base of army operations. This was the start of a thirty-year presence by the army in Yellowstone.

Camp Sheridan grew quickly and by 1910 there were more than three hundred soldiers as well as a large number of civilian employees of the park and its concessions. During this period many of the large hotels, restaurants, bridges and roads were built. Tourism increased dramatically after the cavalry entered Yellowstone

However, for the army patrols, the vast Yellowstone wilderness needed to be travelled on foot or horse. Its elevation, rugged mountain passes and long winters resulted in some of the park patrols being called the "snowshoe cavalry." The mountain wilderness was challenging but the army soon asserted itself throughout the park and was able to bring relative order to Yellowstone.

In 1916 Congress created the National Park Service, a civilian agency, to manage Yellowstone, Yosemite and

P.W. Norris dressed in his Civil War army uniform. Norris was the second superintendent of Yellowstone National Park and was the first person to be paid for the position.

other designated parks. The army left Yellowstone a couple years later. The army preserved Yellowstone until an infrastructure could be developed to manage this wilderness. Parks were a new idea, and the army allowed for a transition to be made from chaos to management.

There still are vestiges of the army's presence in Yellowstone. For instance, the contemporary uniforms of park rangers still bear a resemblence to the army uniforms of the time. The ubiquitous flat, brimmed hat is a direct decendent of period army hats and other examples abound as well.

Above: Large army unit (Minnesota National Guard) at Yancey's Station in 1897. Frank J. Haynes is riding the lead horse.

Opposite Top: Guard duty at Roosevelt's camp in Yellowstone.

Opposite Bottom: Soldier and horse jumping hurdle at Mammoth Parade Ground. The soldiers are lifting their legs to encourage the horse to clear the hurdle.

Surely our people do not understand even yet the rich heritage that is theirs. There can be nothing in the world more beautiful than the Yosemite, the groves of giant sequoias and redwoods, the Canyon of the Colorado, the Canyon of the Yellowstone, the Three Tetons; and our people should see to it that they are preserved for their children and their children's children forever, with their majesty beauty all unmarred.
Theodore Roosevelt, 1903.

Above: Construction of Roosevelt Arch at Gardiner, Montana. Scaffolding and construction materials can be seen.

Opposite: Tourists climbing in the Grand Canyon of the Yellowstone.

Our great National Parks are sections of the old American wilderness preserved practically unchanged. They are as valuable, acre for acre, as the richest farm lands. They feed the spirit, the soul, the character of America.

Who can measure the value, even to-day, of a great national reserve such as the Yellowstone Park? In twenty years it will be beyond all price, for in twenty years we shall have no wild America. The old days are gone forever. Their memories are ours personally. We ought to understand, to know, to price and cherish them.
Northern Pacific Railroad, Brochure, 1920.

Above: First passenger train at Gardiner Depot. The Northern Pacific Railroad provided access to the northern end of the park. As a result, tourism jumped from 300 people in 1872 to more than 5,000 in 1883.

Opposite Bottom: Elk carcasses await loading at Gardiner Depot.

Pages 72 and 73: Steamboat Jean D at dock on Yellowstone Lake. This boat was launched in 1910 and boasted storm windows and a hardtop rear deck and could carry 150 passengers. Several ferries took passengers between Lake Hotel and West Thumb. Eventually improvements to park roads made the ferry service unnecessary and many of these boats were used for sightseeing excursions instead.

71

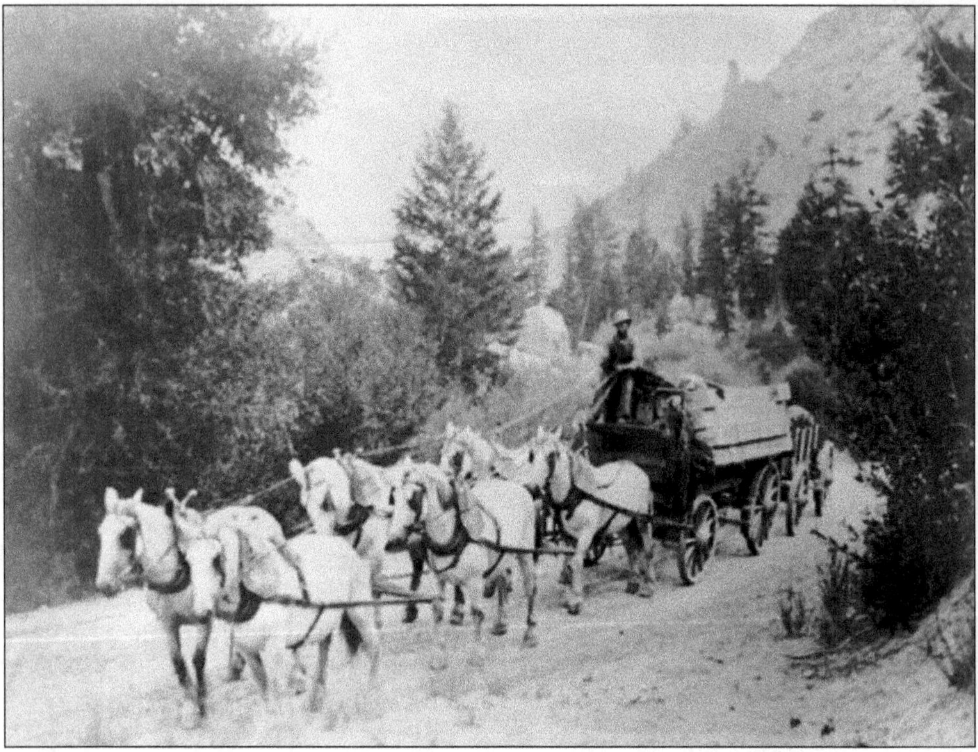

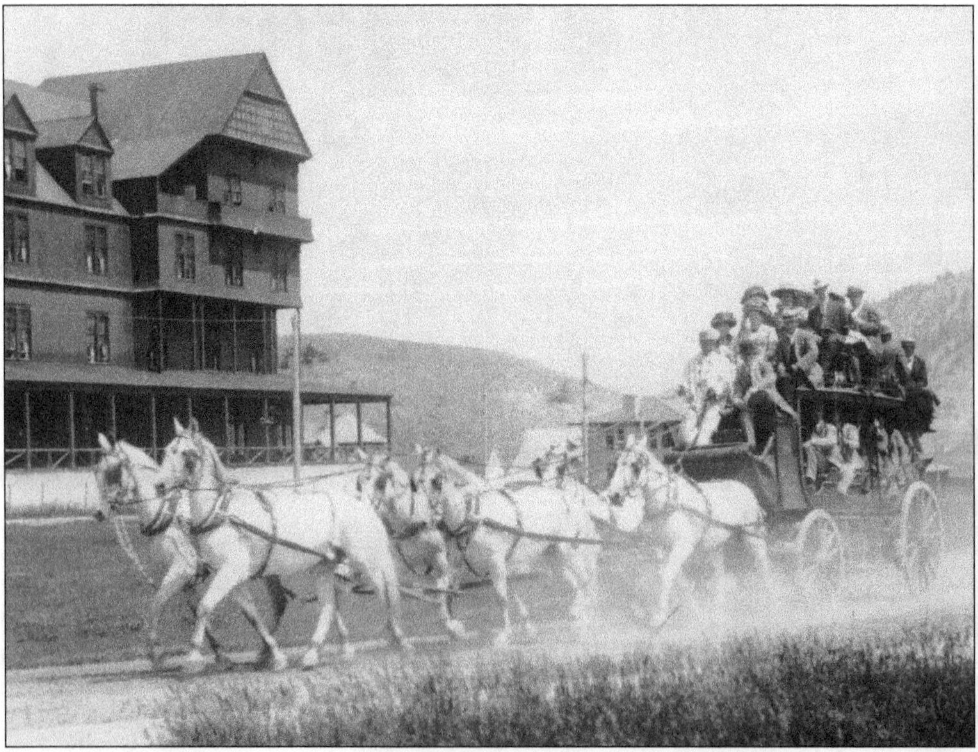

Above: Four-horse coach near Upper Falls. It was customary for men and women to wear fine clothes and fancy hats while sightseeing.

Opposite Top: Six-horse freight wagons near Eagle Nest Rock on Gardiner River.

Opposite Bottom: A crowded Tally-Ho stage coach passing in front of National Hotel. These stages carried twenty to thirty people on each trip.

The stagecoach drivers are grizzled, weather-beaten, full of quaint lies and mysterious quips and jests that none but they understand.
Frederick Dumont Smith, 1909.

Above: Lake Hotel with stage coaches in front.

These passing wagons fill the air with dense clouds of dust which envelop us so that we are scarcely able to distinguish each other. One of the necessities of the tourist in this region is a good linen duster, buttoning well up at the neck, and reaching the knees—also a pair of dark goggles to protect the eyes from the dust and the reflections from the white limestone, which are positively injurious, as well as unpleasant.
Charles M. Taylor, Jr., 1901.

Above: Stage coaches at Mammoth Hot Springs Hotel.

Have you ever seen a real stagecoach? With its four horses, harness rattling, the whip cracking, circle up to the hotel and come to a stop at the exact inch—the driver with his slouch hat inclined rakishly, foot on the brake, and the general air of "Watch me and see how easy it is!" So that morning, when we awoke in Yellowstone, in that sparkling atmosphere, and saw the big red coach come dashing up to the platform...we felt a flow, a thrill of anticipation, that no mere railroad trip could possibly give.
Frederick Dumont Smith, 1909.

Fires of big logs are kept going constantly in the large fireplaces, and every evening a massive, specially-made, swinging corn popper is brought into play and guests regaled with popcorn passed around in a large dishpan.
Olin D. Wheeler, 1905.

Above: Old Faithful Inn lobby. The massive fireplace was constructed with 500 tons of local stone.

Above: The spectacular Old Faithful Inn was designed by Robert Reamer. It took more than a year to build and was finished in June, 1903. Originally this log building had 140 rooms but over the years several additions expanded its size. Large windows in the lobby faced the geysers to the delight of guests. Robert Reamer once said "It was my ambition, to construct a building without a piece of planed wood in it. In all the big structue there is not a foot of smooth finished board or molding."

The work of construction was slow and tedious. Hundreds of miles of forest was searched for gnarled and twisted branches and trunks of trees. Nature's forest cripples were collected by the thousand and the odd freaks of tree growth were seized upon and made part of the big hotel. The balustrades of the staircases are of gnarled branches. The newels and pillars of twisted trunks. Logs everywhere, and the oddest and most fantastic have entered most prominently into the architect's intricate scheme of interior decoration.

W.H. Merriman, describing the construction of Old Faithful Inn, 1905.

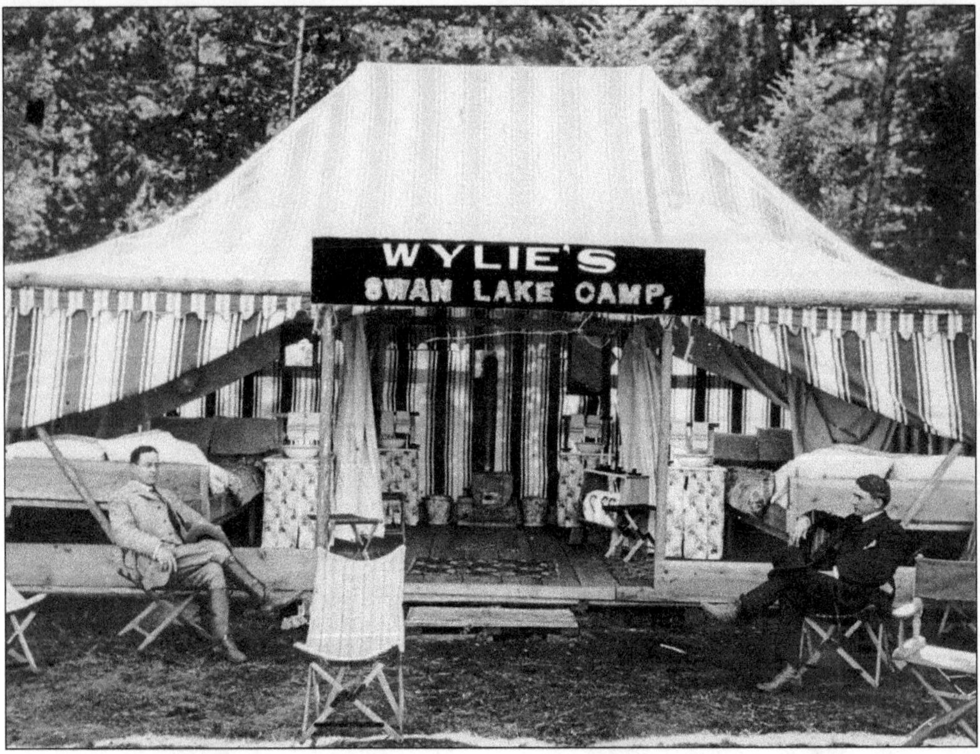
WYLIE'S
SWAN LAKE CAMP,

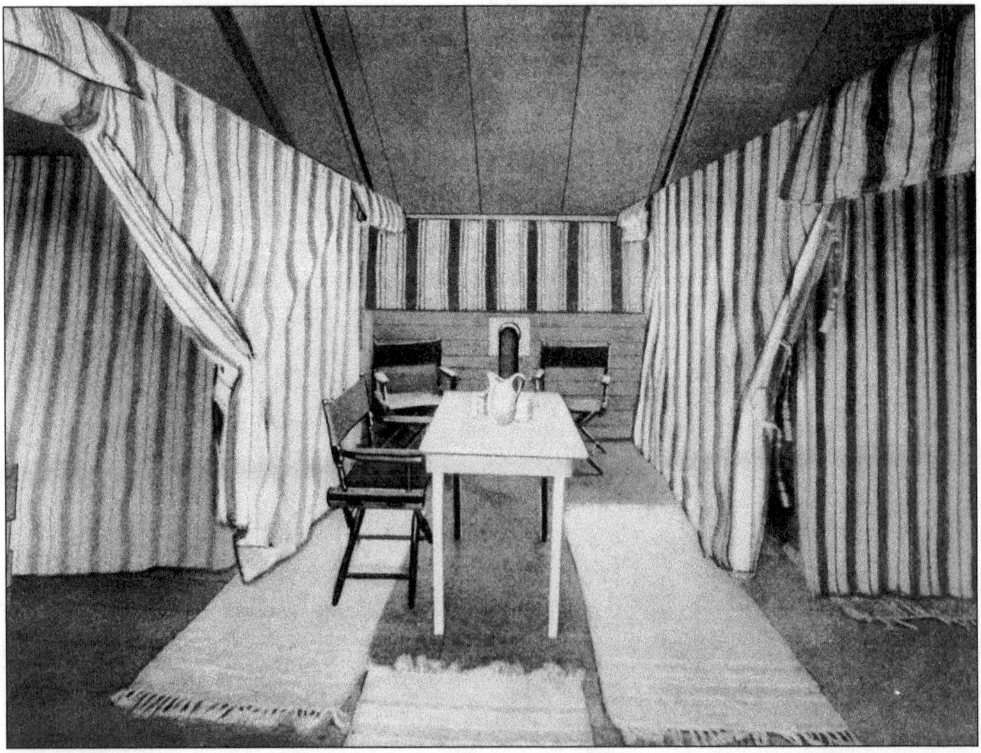

Opposite Top: Two men reclining on folding chairs outside the characteristically striped tents of Wylie's camps.

Opposite Bottom: Sketch of Wylie tent interior. This drawing was captioned "All sleeping tents are heated by a quick-burning wood stove. Fires are built thirty minutes before 'rising bell.'"

Above: Part of Wylie Upper Basin Camp.

During the first evening in camp, we were greeted with right good will by the party around the campfire. We all indulged in delicious white popcorn that had been freshly popped in huge poppers over the campfire. We were entertained by the "savages" (Park employees) with recitations, impersonations and songs.
Dorothy Brown Pardo, 1911.

Above: A bell hop with a full dolly of suitcases.

Opposite Top: Diver and swimmers at Mammoth swimming pool. The pool water was diverted from the Mammoth Terraces, 1925. The pool was decomissioned in 1950.

Opposite Bottom: Loch Leven German Brown Trout caught by Mammoth Hotel bellhops.

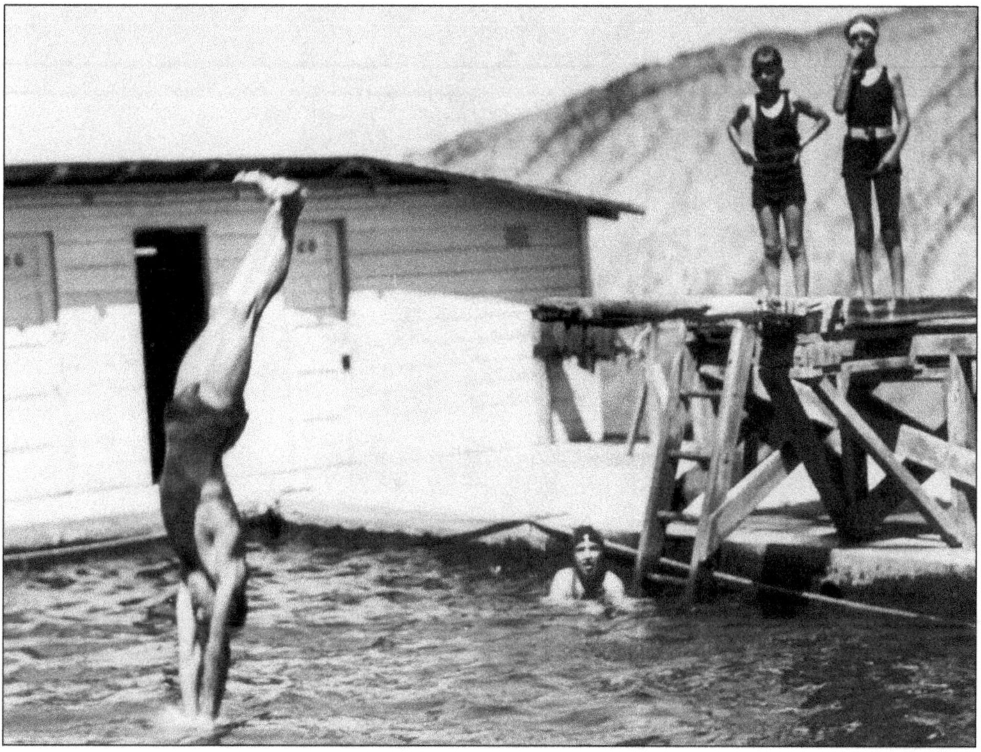

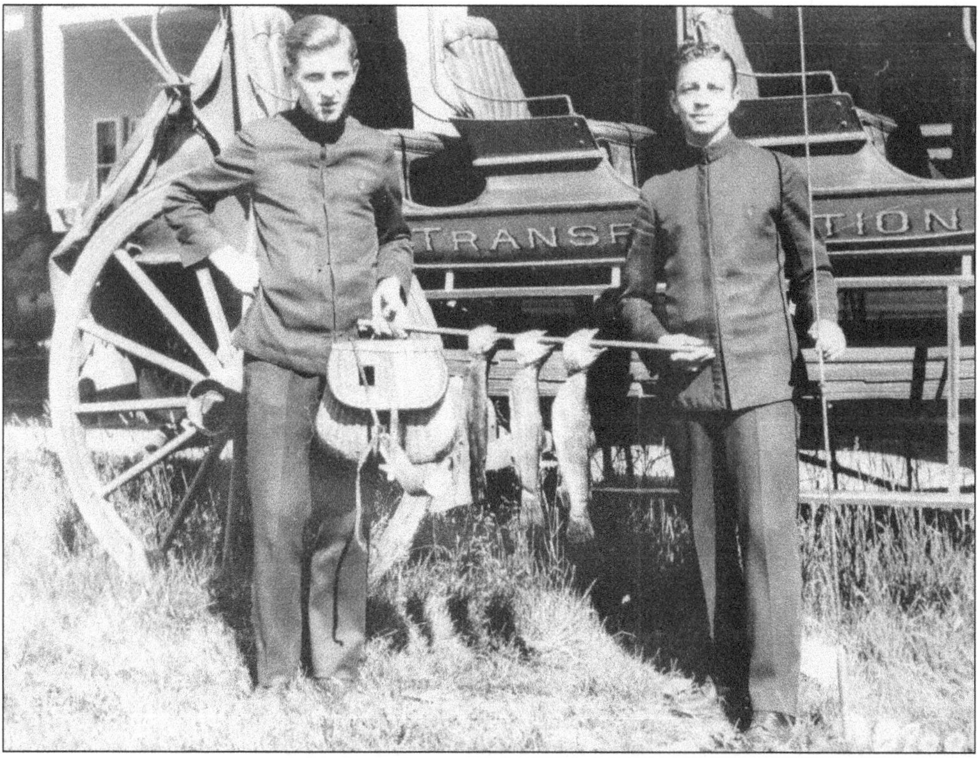

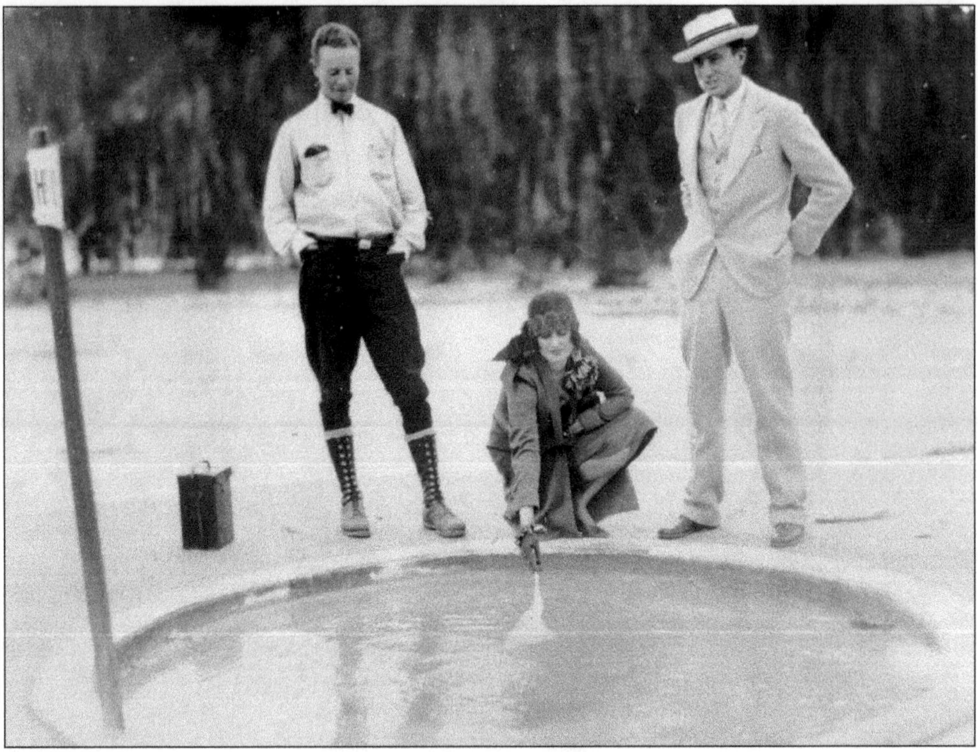

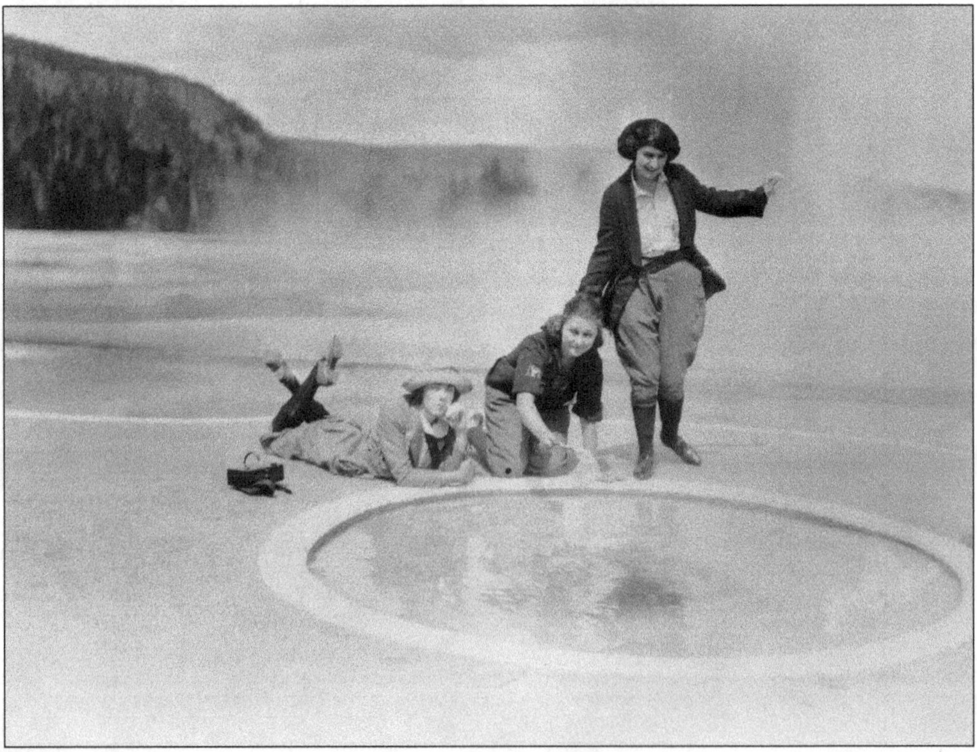

Opposite Top and Bottom: At one time, Handkerchief Pool was a popular attraction at Yellowstone. It is located in the Black Sand Basin and tourists would throw handkerchiefs into the pool that would be sucked out of sight and then recycled back into the pool. In 1929 the pool became clogged and the practice of throwing things into it became illegal.

Above: Fishing Cone had the unique feature of allowing fish to be cooked without taking them off the hook. Many believed trout congregated near the Cone where the water was warmer.

Opposite: Captain Anderson with a chained bear cub on a tall post. For decades it was common practice for the park to keep captive bears.

Above: Soldiers posing with the heads of bison that were confiscated from poacher Edgar Howell. His arrest led to much public outcry and stiffer animal protection laws, 1894.

The most objectionable of all game destroyers is, of course, the kind of game butcher who simply kills for the sake of the record of slaughter, who leaves deer and ducks and prairie-chickens to rot after he has slain them. Such a man is wholly obnoxious; and, indeed, so is the man who shoots for the purpose of establishing a record for the amount of game killed.

President Theodore Roosevelt, 1903.

Opposite: Photographer J.E. Haynes on skis in front of antlers at Mammoth.

Above: Soldiers on ski patrol headed to Fall River. They called themselves the "snowshoe cavalry" and accessed remote areas of the park on skis and horses.

Left here (Old Faithful area) for the post (Fort Yellowstone) the Sunday before Thanksgiving…I made 26 miles the first day, staying all night at Norris Station. The next morning it was 22 degrees below zero, but I pulled out for the Post, which I reached about two P.M. after a cold hard ride of 20 miles. There is something about life in the wilderness that fascinates me. I saddle my beast, and go off on long rides through the forest where everything is so quiet that one can almost hear the solitude.
Private Edwin Kelsey, December 3, 1898.

"MODERN" YELLOWSTONE

As Yellowstone matured, it struggled to keep pace with its crushing popularity. Perhaps the most significant change was the decision in 1915 to allow personal cars into the park. Soon a network of rough roads and bridges were built to handle the traffic. Gas stations and diners began to dot the park to service this growing population of visitors.

Between 1933 and 1942 the Civilian Conservation Corps (CCC) developed much of Yellowstone's modern infrastructure. During this period most of the visitor centers, roads and campgrounds were built. The CCC was a public work relief program that employed unskilled young men to work on rural development projects such as improving Yellowstone. This New Deal initiative left an indelible mark on the national parks.

After WWII, families started visiting parks in record numbers. Tent camping and RVs became popular and affordable for many Americans. Summer vacations in the national parks became a pursuit of the middle-class and the popularity of the parks grew to staggering levels. The parks became destinations and generations grew up spending their summers shuttling between them. Experiences such as *Junior Ranger* programs and ranger-led campfire talks became a rite of passage for many children. Yellowstone allowed ordinary people the opportunity to experience wilderness while being supported with a range of interpretive programs and ammenities they desired.

Yellowstone has always raised controversy and nowhere was this more apparent than in the changing attitudes towards stewardship of its natural resources. Non-consumptive wilderness appreciation gradually became policy and laws to protect the park were developed and strengthened. Intrusive and destructive practices such as stocking of the lakes with non-native fishes was phased out in the fifties. Rangers stopped allow-

Lodge company employee sitting on luggage holding a box camera, 1924. Many seasonal employees returned year after year for the opportunity to live and work in the Park.

91

ing bears to be fed and enforced strict wildlife protection laws. In 1995, almost seventy-five years after the last of Yellowstone's wolves was eradicated, the Grey Wolf was reintroduced. Elk and other large prey species had increased dramatically in number once the wolves were gone and soon overgrazed and Yellowstone suffered widespread degradation. Since the reintroduction of wolves and other initiatives, a more natural balance has been restored and the health of many species has improved throughout the park.

The few surviving bison in the west avoided extinction by seeking refuge in Yellowstone. At the turn of the century there were fewer than fifty bison in the original Yellowstone herd. It was the last free roaming herd in North America and their numbers were gradually increased to more than 3,000 through feeding and predator control. As ranchlands spread around the perimeter of the park concern was raised about the possibility of bison infecting cattle with brucellosis. In 1997, 1,100 bison were slaughtered because they were feared to be carrying brucellosis. Managers continue to grapple with the difficulties of maintaining animals that roam beyond the park's boundaries.

Yellowstone has had to balance development with the management of a vast wilderness. It was a pioneer in many respects and its experiences, both good and bad, were studied at many other parks around the world. Concerns about the impact of tourism, invasive species and adaptation to the warming climate continue. In 1976 Yellowstone was designated an International Biosphere Reserve and a UN World Heritage Site in 1978. Yellowstone is the world's first national park and one of its greatest.

Above: Yellowstone Park Transportation Company buses, Lincolns and touring cars at Mammoth. A fire in 1925 destroyed many of this companies buildings as well as 93 vehicles.

Gliding down the western slope through the cool, silent forests affords an indescribably keen enjoyment, and the motorist must have travelled far who has experienced roads as well built and maintained as this, more than a mile and a half above sea-level in the midst of rugged mountain summits.
Charles J. Beldon, 1918.

Opposite: Debris retrieved from Morning Glory Pool, 1950. In Yellowstone's early days it was common for visitors to drop handkerchiefs and coins into the pools. Several pools eventually became plugged by debris and this practice was discouraged, 1950.

Above: Twenty-five passenger touring car used by Wilbur A. Skaar to carry visitors in Yellowstone.

Pages 96 and 97: A tourists car with a bedroll tied to the fender and a canvas cover to shelter provisions. Yellowstone was opened to car traffic in 1915 and became a popular destination.

When, however, the whir of the motor as it toils up the rugged heights of Mt. Washburn, and passes almost unnoticed within two hundred yards of a band of the most wary of wild animals, the Rocky Mountain sheep, and when at night the bears, having feasted on "beefsteaks that have proved too tough for the tourists," make bold actually to clamber into the motor-cars and despoil seat cushions in search of sweets unwittingly left in side pockets, it will be appreciated that the contention that the motor-car would frighten these animals was quite without foundation. The whole atmosphere of Yellowstone seems to exert a soothing effect on both man and beast, and it is said that "Even broncs won't buck in the Park."
Charles J. Beldon, 1918.

The cañon is so tremendously wild and impressive that even these great falls cannot hold your attention. It is about twenty miles long and a thousand feet deep,—a weird, unearthly-looking gorge of jagged, fantastic architecture, and most brilliantly colored.
John Muir, 1885.

Above: Tourists in a touring car visiting Inspiration Point, which overlooks the Grand Canyon of the Yellowstone River.

Pages 100-101: Parking for Easter Sunrise Service at Mammoth.

The walls of the cañon are of gypsum, in some places having an incrustation of lime white as snow, from which the reflected rays of the sun produce a dazzling effect, rendering it painful to look into the gulf.
Lt. Gustavus C. Doane, 1870.

Above: Tourists fishing off Fishing Bridge at Yellowstone Lake.

Opposite: Releasing hatchery-grown fish to restock lakes. Starting as early as 1881 Yellowstone was stocked for the "benefit" of sport fishers. This practice led to many problems, including the introduction of invasive species such as Lake Trout. As a result of these practices managers have struggled to preserve the park's indigenous fish species ever since.

Pages 104 and 105: Superintendent Albright at the 1872-1922 Yellowstone Golden Anniversary on a dais draped with American flags, bison skulls, elk antlers and moose antlers.

Long dashes down stream taxed my unsteady footing; the sharp click and whirr of the reel resounded in desperate efforts to hold him somewhat in check; another headlong dash, then a vicious bulldog shake of the head as he sawed back and forth across the rocks. Every wile inherited from generations of wily ancestors was tried until, in a moment of exhaustion, the net was slipped under him. Wading ashore with my prize, I had barely time to notice his size—a good four-pounder, and unusual markings, large yellow spots encircled by black, with great brilliancy of iridescent color—when back he flopped into the water and was gone. However, I took afterward several of the same variety, known in the Park as the Von Baer (sic) trout, and which I have since found to be the Salmo fario, the veritable trout of Izaak Walton.
Mary Towbridge Townsend, 1897.

Here at Mammoth where the hot springs "manufacture" many local clouds, and often fill the air with frost crystals, someone may some time be fortunate enough to see a complete solar halo.
William E. Kearns, 1937.

Above: Bombardier snowcoaches at Old Faithful, 1958.

Opposite Top: Snowplane at Swan Lake. This two-person vehicle used a small rear-mounted airplane engine and propeller.

Opposite Bottom: Motorized tobogan at Mammoth.

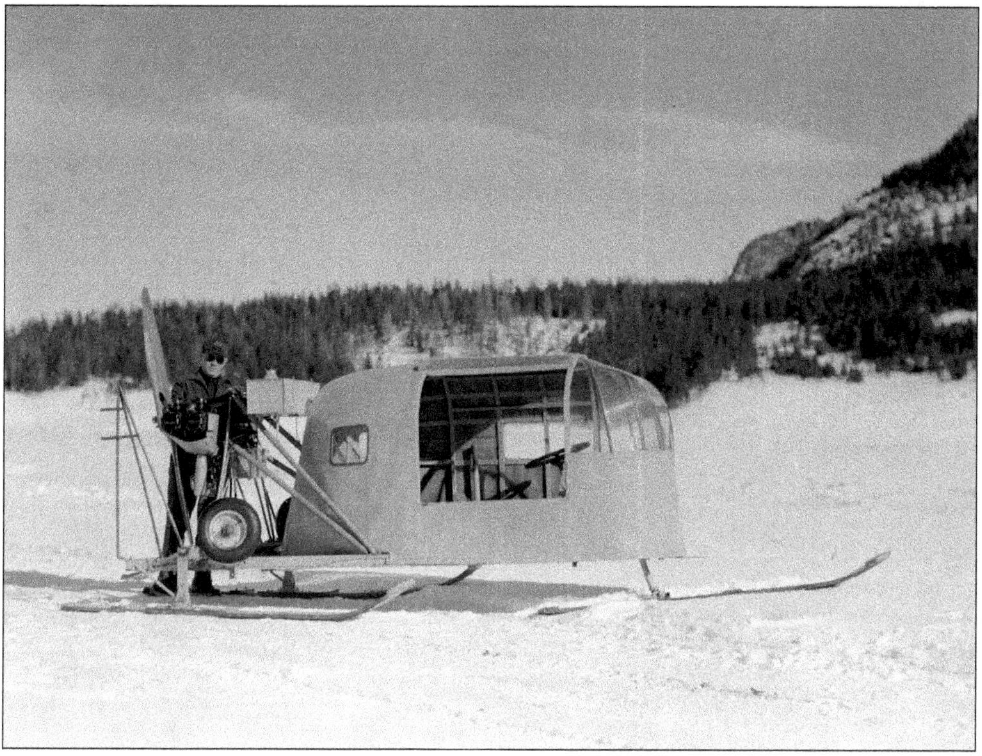

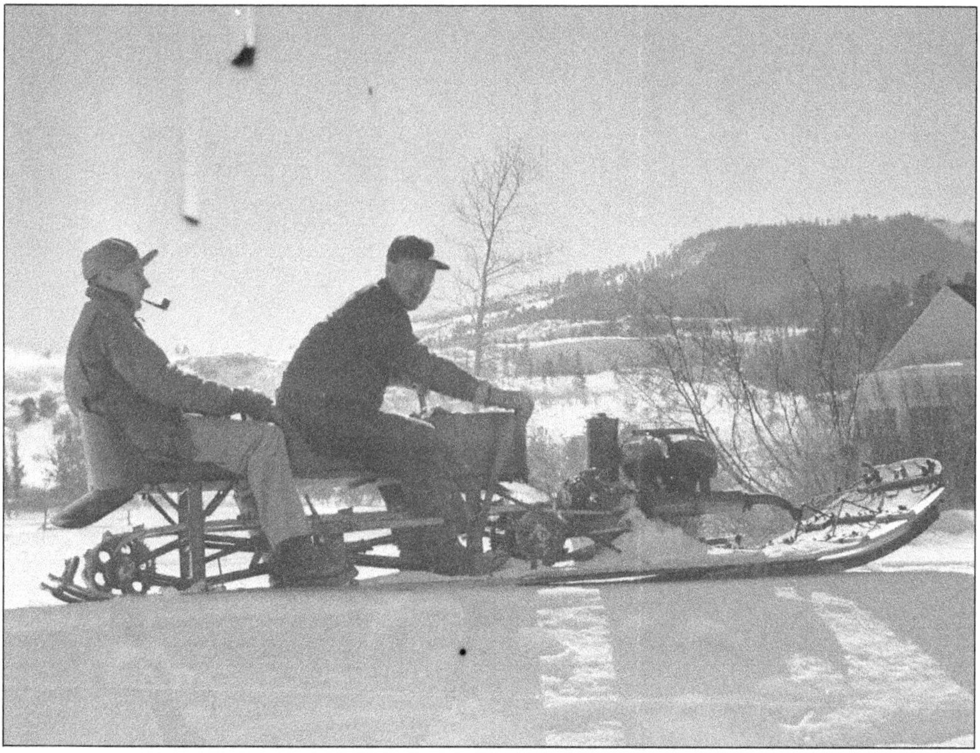

Opposite: George Ross, a park ranger at Old Faithful Ranger Station, 1925.

Above: Crow Chief Max Big Man and daughter Myrtle at Giant Geyser. Chief Big Man is wearing a ceremonial feather headdress and striped trade blanket.

The Yellowstone National Park was the first national park of the great system of national parks to be created by the Congress. In the organic act of its establishment of March 1, 1872, it was specifically "dedicated and set apart as a public park or pleasuring ground for the benefit and enjoyment of the people." Since that time repeated attempts to utilize its wonderful streams and lakes and waterfalls for commercial uses have been made. Fortunately, all have been frustrated. The United States should be the last one to attempt to mar or destroy any portion of this maginficent wilderness area, perhaps the most important natural heritage we can preserve for posterity in this country.
Secretary Ray Lyman Wilbur, rejecting a development request, 1931.

There still remains, even in the United States, some areas of considerable size in which we feel that both red and gray (wolves) may be allowed to continue their existence with little molestation...Where are these areas? Probably every reasonable ecologist will agree that some of them should lie in the larger national parks and wilderness areas: for instance Yellowstone and its adjacent national forests...Why, in the necessary process of extirpating wolves from livestock ranges of Wyoming and Montana, were not some of the uninjured animals used to restock Yellowstone?

Aldo Leopold, 1944.

Above: *Park ranger with a raven on his shoulder.*

Opposite: *W.O. Owens riding a bicycle in 1933. Owens toured Yellowstone fifty years earlier in September 1883.*

Page 112: *Tower Falls as it appeared to the Hayden Survey of 1871 and much as it appears today.*

www.ingramcontent.com/pod-product-compliance
Lightning Source LLC
Chambersburg PA
CBHW060818050426
42449CB00008B/1710